Kingdom Poetry

Volume 1: A Great Awakening

REBECCA TADDEI

First Printing

Kingdom Poetry
Volume 1: A Great Awakening

ISBN 978-0-9853893-2-1

Published by
Goldfinch Oracles, LLC
113 N. 1st Street
McAlester, OK 74501

The Publisher's aim is to produce books for the edification and building up of the Kingdom of God. The Publisher does not necessarily agree with every view expressed by the Author or interpretation of the scriptures. It is left to the Reader to make his/her judgment in the light of their understanding of God's Word by the Spirit.

Unless otherwise noted, all scripture quotations are from the *King James Version* of the Bible.

Printed in the *United States of America*

Cover design by Gwen Titsworth
Goldfinch Oracles, LLC

CONTENTS

Back cover photo courtesy of Manda Tyler Photography, Tulsa, OK

FORWARD

Rebecca is a very unique and inspiring young woman with a great call on her life. Out of the depths of victimization and sin, God graciously lifted and restored her; and, only she can express it so well.

It is the bound, tormented and captive people that know what it is to experience a real and lasting restoration of their lives. She is a brand plucked out of the fire. You will hear *The Christ* speak from her lips and His ministry flowing out from her experiences.

As you read and listen, you will experience the *Spirit of God* speaking to your deep, also. Rebecca is one voice that needs to be heard today and I pray you will enjoy her psalms and poetry as much as I have enjoyed watching her growth in the Lord.

Enjoy and Experience Christ's Healing Touch,

Pastor Linda Darnell
November 19, 2012

Linda Darnell Ministries
2227 S. Garnett #105
Tulsa, OK 74129

DEDICATION

This book of *Kingdom Poetry* is specially dedicated to Brenda Campbell, who witnessed many times the manifestation and glory of God in many of these poems.

She was a precious pillar at our church for over 25 years; but, Brenda was more than a church goer, who we saw every week on Sunday. She truly shined with the light of Christ and was a comfort to all who knew her.

Brenda was an overcomer, a grandmother, a mother, a sister, a close friend, a 'den mother' to some, but holds a very dear and precious place in the hearts of many. Though she is greatly missed on this side of the river, we find comfort knowing she is cheering us on in the great cloud of witnesses.

We love you dearly, Brenda, and we shall continue to carry the torch until Christ be made perfect in us.

Brenda Jane Ogden-Campbell
1950-2013

This is the journey of my walk with Christ, through poetry.

Yes, He has borne our grief. Yes, our hurts, sins and many wrongful doings. But, that sacrifice was already made. It is a portion freely given to us that we might be made alive in Him. There is a place in us we cannot hide. A place deep within our spirit we have been unable to run from; a deep cry from inside our layers of wounds that cries for a Redeemer.

There is a secret place deep within the many caves and crevices of the human spirit, body and soul that go untapped. We try to fill it – to bring peace to the waters – we fight for it – trying to restore hope again as we long for its calm. But, I say unto you it is your deep that has been formed and created by the deep of an Almighty God. It is His deep that calls unto you.

Rejoice, O rejected and despised one! For great is the portion for him that lays himself down; for a New Life shall he gain!

John 4:13-15   Jesus said to her, "Everyone who drinks of this water will be thirsty again, but whoever drinks of the water that I will give him will never be thirsty again. The water that I will give him will become in him a spring of water welling up to eternal life." The woman said to him, "Sir, give me this water, so that I will not be thirsty or have to come here to draw water."

Humble Roaring

August 9, 2010

In Your mercy and grace did You find me, Lord.
In all strength and authority have You freed me.
Through all love and desire does my heart beat for You.
Truly, it is my heart's cry to let my life bring honor to You.
If only the world who knew me could see Your hand!
How You are delicately reconstructing my heart.
Then they would know You, Lord!
Then might they so desire to be satisfied in Your arms,
Knowing they are loved and created by You.
Formed are they from before time itself,
Woven by the potter as clay.
Yet, if all the pain of my life,
Would bring but one into the fullness of You, Lord,
I would walk through it again.
Who was I even two years ago?
Lost my identity within my soul's isolation.
Yet, here You tend to me.
Lavish me with peace and comfort,
Speaking words to soothe my heart's distress.
I know more than anything else in my life,
I am Yours.

For, beyond the bruising of my soul,
I feel Your hand planting seeds of life within my being;
Forming and fashioning me into a woman of Your making.
Truly, a tabernacle of Your presence.
Let King David not have been
The only one to write Psalms to You, Father.
Let my life be a sacrifice of praise unto Your name.
I am lesser.
Truly lesser than the least.
But, with humble roaring will I boast of You.

The Lord spoke to me in August 2010, "I am opening you back up."

I had stared many times at poems I wrote before Christ and wondered where my desire to write had gone. It wasn't until a year and a half after I truly came into the Kingdom of God that the Lord spoke this to me. **Humble Roaring** *was the first psalm born thereafter.*

Blooming Sons
(August 18, 2010)

I will praise You again and again.

I will sing of Your goodness now and even then.

For, Your face delights when spiritual truth is in sight.

I will lay down desire, for, it is the cost for the fire.

I sacrifice my heart, for, it is You who created that part.

I owe nothing to the flesh but all to You.

Be all heaven, earth and all praise!

For, in a whisper, You braise even the callused skin;

But, the fire comes burning even where I've been.

Oh, narrow path!

How perfectly You did graph the stars, sun and moon,

For, the Sons of God that are ready to bloom!

Oh, Husband, Maker, Redeemer, and Friend!

I march in You beginning to all with no end.

Fields Of Lavender
(August 15, 2010)

Sing, O virgin vessels!
Wash the hills with lavender's bloom.
Tears of conscience.
Tears as rain,
To wash no more these hills again.
Virgin vessels of purity,
Truth hath washed away all piety.
Glorious lavender that dresses these hills,
Thy fragrance doth satisfy God's holy will.
For, in the bloom bursts forth Your nectar!
A fragrance created by the Perfector.
Tears of laughter and of pain;
Earth lust faded for ethereal gain.
A calm dispensed after the storm;
A hush of tears now is born.

For, tears has flowed from many a cheek,
That one might be made in love, powerful, but meek.
Though the tears that fell many never knew,
As they fell ,God used them as dew to water lavender's hills.
Waters from sacrificed fleshly wills;
That in the end, the Christ would shine.
And, from inward out, then redefine.
A seal in time full of that new wine!
No more to pine.
No more to whine;
But finally, rifts not mine.
Now I see that bloom of spring;
Yet, that bloom is Him!
All heaven sing!

4

Sweet fields below watered by dew,
Dressed in lavender's hues.
Here, rides He;
Robed in righteousness and majesty.
Power is the horse He rides;
Shaking all earth as the moon would summon the tide.
Calling us back from self and sin,
Where worshipful fear is an offering given to Him.
Here it is that we bring our self, our will,
Our want's overflowing brims;
That lavender in our fields will come forth,
With nectars of sacrifice in such blooms of spring.

One of the beloved members of our church got up this Sunday morning to share what the Lord was speaking to her. She shared the Parable of the Virgins who were waiting for the bridegroom. Five were wise and the other five were foolish:

Matthew 25:1-13 Then the kingdom of heaven shall be likened to ten virgins who took their lamps and went out to meet the bridegroom. Now five of them were wise, and five were foolish. Those who were foolish took their lamps and took no oil with them, but the wise took oil in their vessels with their lamps. But while the bridegroom was delayed, they all slumbered and slept. And at midnight a cry was heard: 'Behold, the bridegroom is coming; go out to meet him!' Then all those virgins arose and trimmed their lamps. 8 And the foolish said to the wise, 'Give us some of your oil, for our lamps are going out.' 9 But the wise answered, saying, 'No, lest there should not be enough for us and you; but go rather to those who sell, and buy for yourselves.' 10 And while they went to buy, the bridegroom came, and those who were ready went in with him to the wedding; and the door was shut. Afterward the other virgins came also, saying, 'Lord, Lord, open to us!' But he answered and said, 'Assuredly, I say to you, I do not know you.' Watch therefore, for you know neither the day nor the hour in which the Son of Man is coming.

*She was sharing, not about the coming of a kingdom in the clouds, but, about the desire Christ had for her to commune and give herself fully unto Him. What she shared really ministered to my heart, because, I had always heard about Jesus coming back in the clouds of glory. What she shared was about the intimacy Christ really desired us to have with him, for us to be prepared and ready for Him to come forth in us. I realized how busy I was; how unprepared I was to commune with Him. I realized I had been foolish with my time and that I had not been giving the whole of myself over to Him. As I went home that afternoon, I quieted myself in the Lord and waited patiently for Him to speak with me. I had been so busy, giving the feelings of loss still from the previous relationship, that I was missing what God was trying to tell me. As I quieted myself, he showed me the tears I had been crying throughout my whole shattered life and how He never lost even one of them. **Fields of Lavender** is a vision the Lord gave me during that afternoon. The 'virgin vessels' are the virgins who have prepared themselves to be truly holy and set apart unto Him.*

Order Flows
(August 13, 2010)

Order flows from the house of the Father.
Chaos runs naked and undressed.
Rubies are the lips of His bride;
Sealed with pendants of Alabaster,
Gifts she brought filled with tears.
Alabaster pendants displayed for all to see.
The fragrance of brokenness mended eternally.
Sweet perfume of heaven these were;
For, time with the Master had formed these for her.
Order flows from the mouth of the Father.
Self runs naked, stripped bare for all to see;
For, order from the Father yields truth,
Rather than shrouds of calamity.

Cinnamon, aloe, sweet oils dress her skin.
For, the presence of the Father purified her from within.
The glow of immortality radiates about her face and robes
Of righteousness dance around her with a humble grace.
Choirs of angels and pioneers of old singing,
"Tears of sacrifice she came in pendants of alabaster,
Your bride is bringing! She has paid the price! Glory!"
Reaping Spirit not Self is her story.

Order has always flowed from the throne room of our Father.
Let confusion and Self die today and choose Life,
For, the later is now!

During the summer of 2010, I had been in a relationship with a man. At the time, I believed it to be everything I had ever dreamed of and more. However, the Lord began to deal with me regarding this relationship.

This man was not who God had for me. The Lord further showed me that he was everything I had hoped for myself; and, that I could choose to be with him, but, that it would not be His best for me. I wrestled with this for several weeks. At the time, I did not know if I had the courage to give up such a seemingly perfect relationship. Yet, the more my emotions wrestled with the Spirit of God within me, the more Christ began to talk to my spirit.

Things were not always what they seemed to be. The Lord spoke softly to me and explained that this man represented a kingdom of this world to me. He reminded me of Jesus being tempted in the wilderness by Satan and was offered all the prestige and riches, if He would but bow down. Then, my eyes were opened to see my foundation for this relationship was based on prestige and the hope of riches. That was part of an old me that was beginning to die. Through tears of this realization was this poem written. I wrote it the hour before I made the call to end the relationship and the message came through tears and a quiet release. Part of an old nature was about to begin the process of extermination.

The Heels Of Your Throne

(August 29, 2010)

Who am I that Your sword should pierce me as fire?
For, I am not worthy of even the ash that falls from the sheath.
Yet, I alone stand before You.
I face the heels of Your throne room in loving surrender;
For, I choose, yes, choose to follow the Lamb.
Not for the loaves nor fish that You gave,
But, the glory and honor due You.
I kiss the heels of Your throne;
And, with humbled tears shall I wash Your feet.

With my life shall I hear a new sound.
With my lips shall I roar all the days long.
For, I cover my face with softened hands,
And bow before all heaven's majesty.
For, an aroma of delight do I lay my life down.
Unknown yet to me of this high price I shall pay;
Yet, before this path have You ordered my steps.
Before time was carved, You birthed me in Your order,
And, the gentle whispers of Your Spirit may I follow.
In honor of You does my heart now sing.
For, new psalms to my spirit You bring!

I received a prophecy from my Pastor on August 22, 2010. I wrote it from a tape of the service because the power of God had caused me to go to the floor.

I remember the Glory of God filling every fiber of my body and surrounding me with such force I couldn't stand. Later that day, I got a recording and wrote this down: 'You have a true call of God on your life. I will not share...I will NOT share my glory with man. Rebecca, God said to get ready that in the next six months God is going to cause you to go through a metamorphosis; and, at the end of those six months, you won't even know who you've become, because, you will have changed so much. These next six months are going to be very difficult and don't look and search and question where God is. God says 'I AM the fourth man in the fire!' And, when you come out, you will be a Tree of Righteousness, a planting of the Lord! After these six months you will be as gold.'

The **Heels of Your Throne** *came a week later after the fire began. This was the very beginning of my understanding of His love and His fire.*

To The Prophet
(an Ode to Linda Darnell)

The sacrifice of many upon your shoulders you bore. The heartache of dreams dying, God allowing to be tore. A price never imagined - yet pushed to walk on through, until all that was left from the fire was no longer who you knew. Many years God allowed you to be separated and placed alone. Yet, all in all God was perfecting a temple, a habitation, His beauty and home. Beauty has truly burst forth from the mouth, colored as new wine. For, Truth does flow – a prophetic sound, speaking only of things divine.

I've seen many faces, clenched jaws, with white knuckled fists. Many to accuse relentlessly, understanding only traditional order in lists. Yet, God alone can stand to judge and shall protect His own; and, that sure word from a sure place as His Prophet and from His throne. For, you carry with you many refined jewels, carved from the colors of fire. You were molded, created, purified, until all that remains is His love and desire.

I hear the sound of many voices in the spirit crying out, 'Wake us, Oh Prophet, from our slumber and give us water In this drought!'

Yet, a voice from within you calls, "Choose Life and go no longer without!"

And, through a pulling and uprooting, have yet a handful come about. But, that handful is well able to ascend on that mountain's top, is the very regeneration of Life – the Elect now disciple, until becoming that fertile crop.

11

I heard a message during the first Sunday in September of 2010, while my Pastor was preaching a wonderful word. During that morning service, I remembered being touched so deeply by the story of her walk in Christ. She shared the story of how God called her out of everything she had known and who she thought she was, at that time, and began the journey of building His kingdom within her.

As she preached, tears ran down her cheeks. She shared of the heartache and loneliness she felt. She shared how God, and God alone, wooed her more unto Himself during those times. She spoke of a journey in ministry, that as of that Sunday, neared 30 years and how a handful of those who said they'd follow remained. What stood out to me was when she spoke of a 'handful of corn' who had ascended to the mountain top was enough corn to feed the multitudes still in the valley.

I remember tears swelling in my eyes, as I heard her heart that morning. I came home that afternoon pondering in my heart about how powerful that 'handful of corn' really was. How small it must seem to those who look upon it in the natural, never realizing nor envisioning the potency and potential of the seeds. All afternoon, I was still so moved by my Pastor's story of her journey. I sat down in bed that night and began to commune with the Lord about my Pastor's journey. As I began to talk with the Lord, He began to show me my Pastor in a way I had never seen her.

This poem was written during a vision the Lord gave me that night. I never realized before the price paid to carry a pure word. I never looked at my Pastor the same after this. I had such a tenderness and love toward her, because, I saw a glimpse of the cost for her to be able to be a light to the body of Christ.

The Road Ahead

October 24, 2010

Beautiful are the waters of Your deep.
It is You that called me from a lover's grasp.
You call me toward Your Life,
To set aside my passions and strife,
To follow You and serve You, Lord, my husband.

I cannot see the road ahead;
But, I trust the hand that guides me.
I feel You pushing me onward.
I felt your hand touching the hallow of my hip,
Changing my walk forever.
Here is my sacrifice to You, O lover of my soul.
I take your Spirit within me, not partial but whole.
In return, You are making me to come forth pure as gold.

Beautiful are the feet of those who carry the Good News!
Wonderful is the gift He brings, who wears the Gospel's shoes!

I had finally given in to my strong emotions that I was still dealing with regarding the relationship I had laid down back in August. I allowed myself to speak with him; and once off the phone with him, I found myself suddenly rushing to the bathroom. As I sat stuck in the bathroom, God spoke so loudly to me, "I am opening your bowels".

I knew that what was happening to my physical body was only a mere representation of what God was really going to be doing to my inner most being. All this happened on a Friday night. All night long and into early Sunday morning, my soul cried out for him. I still felt the pull of my emotions roaring so loudly that I did not know if I could truly continue giving him over to the Lord. I called my Pastor in tears before church service that Sunday. I did not think I had the strength to make it; and I knew I needed to reach out.

She met with me that morning, before church in her office. I was such a wreck. I had felt and experienced the glory of God. I could not deny He was pulling me forward in Him and that He was beginning to raise Himself up in me. Still, the feelings I had for this man were so very real; and, he was so embedded in my thoughts, that I was mesmerized by his fantasy. I shared with my Pastor about the past few months and the anger and rage I had been battling. I scared myself at times and would have to quiet myself in the Lord just to calm the rage down. She ministered to me in love and encouragement that morning.

When service started, I assumed my usual position behind our praise and worship leader as backup vocals. I remember my eyes were closed and I was pushing through my emotional self to enter into worship. Suddenly, I felt the hands of my Pastor on my head and electricity shooting down my body. I found myself under the presence of God completely melted to the floor. I could hear my Pastor praying for me; but, her voice seemed quiet compared to the power of the glory running through and around me. She prayed over me and spoke to the wounds of rape, sexual assaults, and to my tormented spirit. She commanded those degradations to come out of me – they did. I was melted on the floor in front of the whole church, entirely unable to move my body.

Down there I didn't care, because, my heavenly Father was healing my inner most being. I cried, knowing that for the very first time in my 28 years of life, I knew I had actually been a victim as a young girl and I felt my innocence. It was the first time in my life I accepted that. I was always so tough – so accepting of the abuse. I dressed provocatively as a young girl; and coping to the traumas of my youth, I simply learned to blame myself for everything. Yet, that Sunday, the love of Christ pulled out some of those roots; and, all I knew was I was free. **The Road Ahead** *was birthed by the Spirit; after this powerful healing, then followed by* **The Quaking of Your Splendor.**

The Quaking Of Your Splendor

I hear a voice that whispers gently, tenderly,
Softening the screams around me.
I hear the voice of my Husband calling my spirit forward,
Calling my flesh to sacrifice its desires.

But, for love You give, for love You called out.
In earnest passion, You spoke life.
And, redemption now shakes the marrow of my bones.
Though my skin feels light, my strength weary;
On and on do you push, calling Your lover forth.

Oh, Husband, You are my worship,
The hope always longed for, the desire always sought;
And, that which saps me dry when lost.
I have found Your mercy seat, Lord.
Again I call out, kneeling at Your hem, Lord.
I lay my pride down again.
For in the quaking of this splendor,
Face down on knees, I finally surrender.

Fire in my belly, Life flows from my womb.
Laments of sacrifice now bring forth your Spirit's bloom.
Dust falls within my hallows as you touch my hip to follow.
My walk shall not again pride itself in love of men.

On and on I hear you calling,
"Push forward. no time for stalling!"
Steady now to rock beneath,
Which holds me firm under His sheath.
For, in the quaking of this splendor,
Crowns down, no more 'tis I the contender.
Price paid. Life saved.
Forever I shall follow a narrow road paved.

The Prince Was Pricked
(November 12, 2010)

Though my heart was shallow,
Your name is hallowed.
Among thorns a Prince was pricked.
Healing can only be tasted by one who has been sick.

A King is your name!
Your kingdom come and throne shall remain!
No one may point crooked fingers of blame;
For, You never change, Lover, You are the same!
Oh, healing wings that do much more than surround;
They illuminate the very jewels of Your crown.
I stand before a Holy God.
I stand in awe.
I stand in power.
I stand called forth in this very hour!

How in love am I,
With He who ruled the seas!
The twinkle in my eyes
Is but a fragment of who He is to me!
In the midst of the rumble,
Made low my pride 'til humble.
In that calm,
In that rain,
Does my healing unfold a freedom of pain,
As I lay down the crowns of all I gained.

"What you have walked away from is what you have mastered."
— Pastor Linda Darnell

And as a tender plant do we grow. On this dry, cracked ground did life begin to appear. That a miracle is birthed by the development of that life in the midst of a barren ground; dead earth. That He would make us into His Tree of Righteousness, a true planting of the Lord.

That seed planted in grounds of His choosing is a seed He held in His hand long before His words were even spoken over our dark void. — **A note from my journal**

Still You Called My Name
(November 2010)

There's a place of broken dreams,
A road torn and not foreseen,
While searching for those pastures green.
There's a hope, a twinkling eye
In the child's face seen walking by,
Still dreaming of that lullaby.

In the midst of the dirt of shattered dreams and
Wounds of hurt, still You found me there.
Wilted daisies in braided hair, tears washed from April's rain.
Same old song of burdened pain;
No one left but me to blame.
Still, You called my name.

You took my hand to pick me up,
Offering me water from your cup.
It's not every day a stranger comes along,
Showing you how you went so wrong
Then, shows you how to sing the song.

It's not every day someone could embrace
All the strangeness away from this place,
And forgive the dirty tears from your face.
And no one could take that from me.
No not a place, fight or calamity.
For, You have anchored me and let me just be –
Freely, the real me.

"We are either representing God or substituting."
— Pastor Darnell

19

Mercy Undressed The Darkness Of Rain
(February 3, 2011)

It is a place I flee to.
I adhere to a soft fumbling around me.
This breath I take lingers no more the dust
That once coiled around me.
Yet, a fragrance I find.
Warming the air,
This breath I take,
A gasp more or less in a passage of time.
This corridor I am walking is dark walled – narrow.
Yet, a light is glowing,
Among this sweet fragrance it does billow.

I feel a hand guiding me, pulling me onward.
I hear the voice of a lover calling.
It is my savior.
A true lover to my soul.
The voice so long I carried,
Now filled with the feeling summer's hues;
And the strength to withstand the winters.
His breath is within me.
It waters me as a flower with mornings dew.
I hear a rumbling still,
Knowing my earth, this flesh, does shake —
Knowing that my lover is calling us before it is too late.
Many eyes once looking ink have now turned to grey.
If only I had known Him — my Savior,
Then I could have brought a word of life!

But, stand here do I, reminiscing not of the past.
Firmly, though, I move onward.
My Lover hold me tight in grasp.

He alone is the Redeemer.
The one who loves the scorned.
The one who carried you
And desires to show himself through.
He is the Christ.

Where are you wounded, Soul?
Dark hallows promised you bliss?
Where are you treacherous promises?
Promising love if we gave more than a kiss.
Where are you strong arms?
You said you could reach me in my mess.
Dark halls – long falls –
All buried 'neath blood stained brows.

Yet, I say there is a Healer!
One who knows more than your name.
I say there is a tomorrow,
Where mercy undressed the darkness of rain.
I say you are a body!
Colorful you are, so what?
I say your spirit is calling forth,
For the Christ in you to reign!

A Psalm

Don't ever take Your breath away.
Don't ever take away the tears that fall;
For, they are the price of the call.
Don't ever take Your hand from me;
For, in Your correction I am made free.

The Head That Rises

What prize is this, Oh Prince of Peace,
To push through layers of comforting fleece?
A sheep am I lead to the slaughter,
To rise up alive a Son – not daughter.

"Why call me forth?" My past cries out!
"What is this 'gifting' and raucous about?"
Looming, as past fantasies push on,
Will I 'til made whole and free.

Eternities' crown rests on my head,
When I rise again, not alive, but dead,
And flesh finally, fully put under.
No more that old carcass to steal and plunder.

I see a head rising forth from ash,
The Christ appears in me at last!

Secret Storeroom
(July 22, 2011)

Here is my secret storeroom, Oh God.
The milk of delusion, carnal thinking in fog.
Here is my key You handed to me.

Here is my weakness – I give it to Thee.
Here are my stains soiled in shades of red.
Here is my sacrifice, a purging from tainted beds.

Here I take my womb and lay it humbly down,
My arrogant disaster – that which was my golden crown.
For, in me, You are birthing a new order, tried and true,
That will remove the tarnishes of Self, through and through.

An order where Your love alone has begun to anchor,
Within me, Your throne.
A love many may never know,
For, they fear what correction might reveal and show.
Yet, let me be a pillar of light – a pillar of You,
That the world may see correction is what love must do.

During my weekend at Prayer Mountain, the Lord healed me from roots of rape and molestation. Another lovely lady from our church, who had been freed of similar issues years ago, sang a song about the heart. She sang about how Christ gave the key and wanted to go inside a secret room where even she wouldn't go. When He handed her that key, she didn't feel ready to face what was hiding inside. It was a song about opening the secret doors of the heart and allowing God to face those dungeons within us. Little did I know the extent of the start of my healing in this area. This poem came several hours later in my cabin's 'upper' room. No one could take from me the healing Christ did for me that day.

I Turn My Face Aside
(August 6, 2011)

I turn my face aside and unto you;
That you may uncover old patterns I still do.
That your glory might be fully revealed,
And, so this Son will be eternally sealed.

Oh, beauty that calls from within this vessel,
I yield again unto you;
That the identities of many voices are unraveled,
Leaving those around speechless and baffled.
That You, Oh Lord, would bring your Spirit forth in such a way,
That the true gold shines forth before humanity on display.

Oh, that You would choose the vessel most broken
To be living proof of Your love's token.
I join the angels singing,
"Resurrection Life He is now bringing!"

I praise you with the fragrance of my life and
Bless You for cutting the impurities with Truth's knife.
Oh, husband! Oh, Lover of my soul!
I surrender my throne of gold.
I lay down my dreams and self-made grace.
I lay down who I was,
That through me now shall shine your face;
The true Christ in me unblemished and pure,
The hope of humanity now rooted in a place truly sure.

"When the inner becomes the outer and the outer becomes the inner, then, you have entered the Kingdom of God."
— A message from my Pastor

Stewardship Of Grace
(August 2011)

Oh, delicacy! Oh, beauty of the flower!
Oh, Master! Oh, Ruler, You are arriving this very hour!

The gentleness and love that comes by Your lovely grace is,
Yes, a free gift that so many do misplace!
It is a jewel of your eye, taken from a portion of your heart.
It sparkles from your glory light, from your throne never apart!

Many have held this sacred jewel;
Yet, never understood the spiritual rule,
That stewardship is the bow that ties this gift –
This jewel of your eye!

Oh, Earth, hear me proclaim and sing!
It is grace, yes, that covers all sin.
But, wisdom and responsibility is the administration
Of a leader towards humanity.

*"Cast the snake out of the fireplace or you allow the presence of
God to clash with the sterile atmosphere."*
— A message from my Pastor

Rise Up!

So, I say rise up!
Cast off your selfish slumber!
Emotions that bring turmoil,
Throwing to your heaven it's soil.
Trying to remind the throne of chaos not all is gone!
Just yourself to be counted as loss.
In earth of the higher step I up!

I remember my Pastor telling me, in front of our church, that she would not try and keep me should I decide to go. I was hurt and angry, mostly at myself. I had allowed my emotions to spin out of control and it took all I had to even drag myself to the church meeting in Bristow, OK.

See, even Jesus had to come to that place within Him that He would choose the will of the Father. I cried the whole drive home and struggled through the night. When Sunday morning came, I chose to get up and go to church. I knew I had nowhere else to run, because, my vices had been stripped away.

I remember a lovely couple from my church that morning singing 'Refiner's Fire;' and suddenly, my spirit leapt within me. I jumped to my feet, tears flowing down, as I cried out, "I CHOOSE to be Holy! Set apart for You, my Master, ready to do your will!"

By the time the song was over, my legs and ankles were trembling in the anointing. This poem came from that break-through. It was another step in learning to push forward as an overcomer.

Through Brokenness Shall There Be A Banner
(October 2011)

In brokenness I am defined, for here are your visions refined.
Though words seem cutting, harsh and unkind,
The pain comes from a cutting away of places blind.
Here in the brokenness of my heart,
I feel the ground thought solid shaking 'neath my heel,
The growing of a substance hoped,
For, from what ne'er seemed real,
As a layer once again un-denying-ly gets peeled.
Here, in the wilderness, the sounds seem as clamor.
Yet, the Spirit within me whispers Truth, not in stammer.
Here, from the valley, shall soon bring forth a banner.
Beaming forth in beauty, righteousness in Christly manner.

"What is the cost? To lay the soul down."
— Pastor Linda Darnell

I Lay Down Strife

What is this foolishness on my lips?
Idle banter secretly wishing ill conceit?
Mocking and ridiculing, in the form of humors, calm deceit;
Seeds of rejection are in that cup where I sip.

The ridicule of a foolish heart.
How easy we discuss!
Yet, all the while that Light dims down,
The more these lips do fuss.
Where is that Christ we sing about,
When we point our fingers of blame?
Negating all the self-wrought shame.
Oh, how we make that drink more stout!

So, from that cup again we drink,
Until, to ourselves, we feel much better and
Silence, within our being, that red and black letter,
As that seed within wilts and shrinks.
When, Oh, Church, may we rise up,
Taking our place in His vine of a purified life?
In unity, I shall stand and fight to refuse divisions' cup.
In love, be knit and strength shall come,
When I learn to lay down strife!

"We are in the birth pangs of travail. The heirs are being peeled layer by layer. When the Sons of God are free then the world shall be set free!"
— *Pastor Linda Darnell*

Your Embrace
(August 26, 2011)

How can I run into the arms of a man?
How can I find my solace in the warmth of bed?
How can strong arms sustain me any longer?
For, You have loved me with a jealous love!

Your thoughts have continuously been upon me.
Your arms have filled the void within me.
Your face so smiled upon me,
That despair had to run from my heart.
Your eyes saw tears that fell from the loneliness,
Left by flighty past lovers.
Empty wanderers were they.
Ungrounded in their affections,
Only blinded by the lust of their flesh.

But You, Oh Lord, You knew the emptiness I tried to hide.
You knew the depths of my longings for love.
Sacred arms that had to carry me.
Righteous judgment did you display throughout my being,
That all may see Grace does truly abound and
Justice stings only for a moment;
And yet, brings forth eternities seed.
Oh, crown of thorns upon Your head no more,
No more must You any longer bleed.
Indeed resurrection has come and
I'm white as snow indeed!

I can feel the strings of my heart play new tunes;
For, emotion no longer woos
By seducing words and tainted perfumes.

In the midnight hours, a new call I hear.
The gesturing voices now silencing their sneer.
I've heard a voice – one that sounds as the deep,
Calling my spirit onward into eternity's sacred keep.
Oh, billows of earth within me,
How quickly do you crumble
'Neath His voice my idols tumble.
Heaven rejoices for scarlet is redeemed!

A Prayer
(October 21, 2011)

Dress me with garments of love.
Cause me to walk with hands graced with charity.
Let bowels of mercy be a guide and
Let your wisdom be the crowning jewel
As I learn to walk with a humbled mind.
Teach me to understand all of this,
That I may be a bondservant of You.

"God has a much greater purpose than our own personal deliverance! He has tied us to what He is finishing in this earth."
— Pastor Linda Darnell

Emptying The Bottles
(November 17, 2011)

Yet, will I quiet myself in You,
That the torment of my mind shall have no grip nor hold.
Yet, will I give my broken wounds to your palms —
Your threshing floor.
Yet, will I say the perfumes have been dried and
The curtains now drawn closed.
There is nothing but empty bottles around,
Crying out to still be filled.
In bowing myself to You, I break each bottle one by one.
Only You can wipe the dust off my brow.

This is based on the word of the Lord in Hosea, chapter 1 -3. God allowed the oils to dry up, that the wayward wife and mother would be brought back to the love of the Lord, which was her first love.

We cannot see it many times, when we so easily look around and see the desert and how everything has dried up. Yet, the Lord spoke to me in this chapter, while I was going through a particular circumstance. The riches and wealth I laid down when I decided to follow the Lord were trying to woo me back. How easily our minds remind us of the former life and of what we let go. How deceitful our thoughts really are! The pleasures of sin last only for a season; and, in the end, bring us death.

Again, I found myself battling through the thoughts of my past reflection and pushing forward in the things of God. This meant I would have to place my trust in His hands that He would never have me give something up that was nothing more than a counterfeit to His plan. This psalm really came during that process of overcoming.

Sealed with A Kiss
(November 29, 2011)

Whet my tongue with the waters of Life.
Seal my lips with a kiss from the burning coals on Your alter.
Nothing in me shall any longer be mine.
I relent to You, oh, pouring of a new wine.
My heart beats wild as I dance before You.
Though many around, I can see only You.
Refine within me Your time free of age,
As a resurrected life now turns my page.
Oh, birthdays so sweet! A celebration of old,
No longer dwell I on the many years You have told.
For, the spirit within now turns each wheel,
Until inside out, no more dwell I on simply how I feel.
Ah, yes! The mind of Christ!
Push I forward and fight to keep on,
That the rocks who cry out may be silenced in their song.
And here on your alter rise I your perfume,
And melt myself to your Spirit where I eternally belong.

After my Pastor preached about having rocks in our heads, choking out the pure seed of Christ within us, God dealt with me during this particular service about many thoughts that had come to haunt me.

I remember it took everything in me to drive an hour to even make it to this meeting. It was so worth it once I made it; because, though I fought hell to not only get there but stay there, the Lord moved on me in a whole new way and I danced before the Lord, which I had never done before. I danced and danced and was so caught up in the Spirit that my eyes were closed and it was just He and me. A jewel from our church, who had taken me under her wing for a season when I first came to our church, had obeyed God when she grabbed me by the hands and lead me out in the aisle that night. As freedom in the spirit flowed, my mind broke free from the torment. Where there is freedom in the spirit, there is truly liberty.

By the time I came to, I was in front of the whole church and shaking. I had never cared less about what people thought about me in my entire life. I danced purely and lovely before no one but Him. No one else mattered.

The Daystar Is Rising
(December 21, 2011)

What manner of mouth have I,
That I may praise your name?
What banner is this raise I,
Proclaiming you stay the same?
These shackles on feet now, breaking their gain,
No stammering break forth I humbled crowns of fame.
Free to walk, for broken are the curses, that made me lame.
No need to speak in riddle or pun,
Here has breached through the night a Son!
A Daystar rising and casts away the confusion and chaos
That once clouded the day.

My Pastor preached on the wheel of destiny: The wheel of destiny is the potter's wheel! I am a steward of the grace of God.

"You will never understand Son-ship until you recognize the purpose being brought forth in your wilderness; that there is an Israel being formed."

His Songs Over Me
(December 24, 2011)

His songs over me are rejoicing!
His songs over me are love!
His songs over me are rejoicing!
His songs over me are love!

How beautiful are the waters deep!
For His light shines from even there.
A stir in the waters deep,
Resurrect my spirit there!
He sings a song of love over me,
Bringing forth His perfect seed.
He calls to me a song o'er the rain,
For I am His desire and my love His need.
A song is sung, unblemished and pure,
Rejoicing, rejoicing of this I am now sure.
Oh, banner of love how sweet though art.
Oh, bright and morning star,
That you have separated me apart!

An elder at my church called and left a voicemail of encouragement on my phone. It was during a difficult time while my son was hospitalized that my church family took turns calling me to give me a scripture of encouragement.

The scripture was Zephaniah 3:17: The LORD your God is with you, he is mighty to save. He will take great delight in you, he will quiet you with his love, he will rejoice over you with singing.

I was so moved with this, because, I could just picture the songs of the Holy Spirit resounding from within my being towards the air around me. I pictured angels over my son singing songs of love and victory. Something about this rope of strength I had been thrown brought a poem of light from the middle of my midnight hour.

Unwind Yourself In The Fabrics Of My New Nature
(February 2012)

Awake me, oh beauty, longing to be my countenance.
Raise me from slumber's bed.
Peel deception's nest from atop my head,
That I may hear my lover's call.
Desire woven within a hide and vaulted door.
You unwind Yourself in the fabrics of my new nature,
Weaving life as finest silks on priestly robes.
Oh, righteous splendor that undresses illusions of grandeur.
You bathe me in glory, line upon line, precept upon precept.
Heavenly man who now consumes this being,
Call for the vessel of who I was long, long ago.
Cause me to rise no more,
But, die to self that I might live in You.

Ephesians 1:4,5 *For he chose us in him before the creation of the world to be holy and blameless in his sight. In love he predestined us to be adopted as his sons through Jesus Christ, in accordance with his pleasure and will.*

The Tree Of Good
(April 2012)

Oh, Tree of Good, you called aloud,
Calling those from within a crowd.
You said you'd show them truth and life
Living forever like husband and wife.
Yet, you blinded their eyes and hide the truth,
That Christ in us is that fountain of youth.
You only imitate the way of righteousness
And parallel, you run the road of the unjust.
I shall anchor myself to that hope in sure,
And allow the Christ to raise up in me, pure.

The LORD God made all kinds of trees grow out of the ground — trees that were pleasing to the eye and good for food. In the middle of the garden were the Tree of Life and the Tree of the Knowledge of good and evil.

Genesis 2:9, this revelation came in the car on the way to Weatherford, TX. My Pastor called and shared with me a bit of her sermon which was about the 'Tree of good AND evil.' She told me to talk with the Lord and see what He had to say about it. I did; and, the Lord began showing me that those who eat of the tree of good walk a path parallel to those who eat the fruit of evil, because, neither are from the Tree of Life. As I listened to my Pastor preach later that evening, God began to deal with me heavily about the 'good.'

The 'good' on that tree is simply an imitation of outward righteousness; yet, is deluded by an inner strive for perfection. The problem is that, trying to just be 'good' is us losing sight of God's will and putting trust in ourselves. We have, thus, forfeited Life for a counterfeit. God was showing me how I was trying to be a Christian rather than letting Christ rule and reign within me. I had gone astray. Through this revelation, I have allowed God to work his Truth in me rather than settling for my own perceptions of Christianity.

The Deception Of The Church
(April 2012)

Oh, covenants we've made on flowering words;
Vain and idle deceptive little birds.
Their nest of discord had veils over thee,
Mocking delusions disguised as freedom dressed lovely.

We shot up rage.
We shot up insanity.
We shot up illusions of self-made vanity.
We lied to our minds to ease our conscious,

In hoping to walk slightly sinful, yet, appearing to be righteous.
Yet, dare not allow one to dig and find
The truth within us, we long ago did hide,
That which first made us blind.

We've taken the blood Christ, spilled for us,
And created a weapon, a syringe of puss,
And labeled the vials:
'Righteousness,' 'Redemption,' 'Grace,' and 'Faith.'

Yet, we never have been freed from our own denials.
So, to coax our conscious and heal our self,
We grab the vials off the whore's shelf
And infect our brethren with the disease of our blood
And crucify him all in the name of God.

Wake up, oh addict – you who say you are pure.
Remove the needles from religion put in you by her!
Desire truth, seek the Christ
And choose life, for the true redemption is now!

Revelations 17:1-6 *One of the seven angels who had the seven bowls came and said to me, "Come, I will show you the punishment of the great prostitute, who sits by many waters. With her the kings of the earth committed adultery, and the inhabitants of the earth were intoxicated with the wine of her adulteries." Then the angel carried me away in the Spirit into a wilderness. There I saw a woman sitting on a scarlet beast that was covered with blasphemous names and had seven heads and ten horns. The woman was dressed in purple and scarlet, and was glittering with gold, precious stones and pearls. She held a golden cup in her hand, filled with abominable things and the filth of her adulteries. The name written on her forehead was a mystery: BABYLON THE GREAT, THE MOTHER OF PROSTITUTES AND OF THE ABOMINATIONS OF THE EARTH. I saw that the woman was drunk with the blood of God's holy people, the blood of those who bore testimony to Jesus."*

A Psalm

(June 30, 2012)

Let all that is within me know and be antiquated.
For, You have formed me in the beginning,
And shall form me in the latter.
I shall be Yours, I shall resemble you.
For, You wove me – intimately in the spirit.
Wooed my bosom to long only after You.

Your love anchors me deep,
And, though cry out I, You hold me fast,
That I might not fall back into slumber.
Dragon's teeth gnash at me and my sons.
But, we belong to and are forever redeemed.
The shadows may stalk but cannot conquer.

For, we are strewn out in fabrics made of iron,
Forged by the indwelling of Your Spirit.
I shall ponder upon Your goodness.
But, Your mercies have overtaken me.
I am consumed by Your everlasting light.
For, I shine forth now glimmers of what soon shall be all of You.
I lay me down again.

A Light Universal Pondering

Is it not for me to wonder that You created all things beautiful and wonderful? That every subatomic particle creating fields of mass versus utter obliteration of mass itself is all Your work. How beautiful did You form the 10 billion stars of the *Milky Way* and place us among the stars ¾ distance from the center! How perfect the development of the *Andromeda Galaxy*! You gave it to us that we might wonder amounts of years for our galaxy to expand into it. Yet, You are the sun of our galaxy and the Higgs Boson particle that creates mass itself on a subatomic level.

No mind can fathom the greatness of You. My mind is feeble to understand the greatness and depth of Your love. Your ways are perfect and You are spirit – alive in me. Raise the banner of Christ within me. That You may be the bright and morning star that never shall go super nova, for, You are eternity and depth of the universe itself. You hold the key of significance. Holy are You husband and creator of my spirit and all that is merely fathomed in all its complexities.

The whispers of Your spirit seem as Doppler shifts many times as I try to analyze your voice and study to understand light that still remains in many places as great distances from my point of origin. Yet, the more I seek you – the more I lay down, Your radiations reach for me and uproot me towards You. Yet, I am finding that light, in all arrays of spectral analysis, is really the beauty of You forming Your will in me. You are beautiful, my Lord, in all ways. Be beautiful and made perfect in me.

Take the reconstructed idols and hidden animosities. Take the frost from within shattered places of my heart and restore me by the warmth of Your love and affections, as I return to You. My name is in Your hand; and, the name of Baal shall be removed from my lips. Let the vaults of perfume dry up, that the oils of Your presence might saturate my skin with Your fragrances.

To Let You Shine In My Place
(July 14, 2012)

The beauty of my youth again; I lay it down, down, down,
And take the dust back to the ground, ground, ground.
I take my heart in Your hand to remove the clay,
Though I know not tomorrow – I give it to You anyway.
Here in my solace, I know You're here,
Though You make me search for You,
Love whispers still in my ear.
How can I depict a man perfect right and true?
When You alone know the heart and see all he shall ever do?
Will he lay himself down to You choosing You over me?
Will he sell himself to Your purpose with unmapped certainty?
Will he know Your love above my own;
And, search You with all his heart?
Or, will he build an idol out of youth and in vanity soon depart?
I give You all the blessed graces You gave me upon this face.
But, I choose to lay it down again,
Allowing You to shine in its place.
I choose to take the idol down of all such vanity.
That You may reign in me,
Your son, as I learn to walk in liberty.

I let go of a friend I had known for 17 years when this poem was written. There had always seemed to be a connection and I wanted desperately to make the friendship work as a relationship. The Lord allowed me to make my choice; and, as I began living with it, I quickly realized I had made the wrong one.

I had been in a major battle and was worn down. Rather than immersing myself in the presence of the Lord, I fought to drown the depression out by other means. It was the wrong timing, wrong person, wrong motive, wrong everything; and, I had to forcibly snap myself out of it, or, I felt I'd quickly begin to retract back even farther.

Everything begins in our mind. It is a playground for calamities. I also know, that sometimes, we just have to make a bad choice; and, those around us have to take a step back and just allow God to deal with us. Well, He did. This poem was birthed from another layer of desperation and loneliness being stripped from my soul.

After this poem was written the Lord spoke to me, "I was yours from the beginning."

It was my spirit to the Lord's and vice versa.

I Am Going To Places Man Has Not Seen
(July 22, 2012)

I am going places man has not yet seen;
For, it only belongs to those who truly believe.
I have been awakened from slumber,
And am learning to live un-encumbered.
Here am I – to be Your jewel.
As You polish away all scratches of 'cruel,'
That I may be Yours whole.

A vagabond by nature is the carnal way.
But, in the stillness, I hear the faint whispers say,
"Hold on, there is another way!"
So, shake off your slumber, oh dreary one,
And arise in Me and I in you as one.
That conformity shall entwine your will to Mine,
And unblemished, you shall be My Rhine,
For, I speak to you in songs divine,
And, I alone press you to form new wine.
So, chase off the daydream of past times;
For, I was yours always and always you were mine.

*"You'll never get away from who you are; so, it's time to let
Christ shine through you. You are just on a journey of overcom-
ing. We need to stop allowing the money changers and thieves to
enter in through our circumstances and rob from us. They enter
in and only bring death."*
— A message from my Pastor

Abba Father
(August 31, 2012)

You are Abba Father,
Not my departer.
You are the resurrector – my insurrector.
My inner conscious bequest,
That in this life may I pass that test,
Which puts You first all I do,
That Your glory and life might wholly shine through.
Oh, Abba Father, that Your name shall be sealed on these lips,
That the marrow shall be changed,
Within the hallow of these hips.
Oh, wine divine - so sublime!
Is this resurrection of eternity's time-line?

Prayer Mountain: The Lord told me He would remove the name of Baal from my lips and place upon them Abba Father. He asked me if I'd be a lamb for my generation; and, I said yes, I will go.

Hosea 2:17 For I will remove the names of the Baal from her mouth, and they shall be remembered by name no more.

Oh Age

Age has been a curse upon the face of Your people.
Hurting and torn, oh Lord, their eyes sink in sorrow.
Abandoned by love and engulfed in themselves,
Antiquated in their very morrow.
Beauty is a deceptive garland worn by many a youth.
Secured only by the reflection they see in the mirror of the mind.
Vanity is seductive, an elusive type of birth.
For, it tapes the wounds, masks the hurt,
And builds until one is blind.

Strong Tower
(October 17, 2012)

A strong tower ministry is who You are to me.
A fortress of refuge hides me eternally.
You are the rock on which I stand,
For, weakness was found by the hands of man.
How can I turn to the side,
When narrowly You lead Your true bride?
For, I see around me bitter crumbs,
Leftover from flesh eating bums.
Oh, King of the humble, how secretly You would
Until the passions of my flesh are conquered, not subdued!
Father me, oh Prince of galaxies and
Developer of universal mysteries.
Lead me to be bound by love;
Called out in love rooted in love
Enfold me into Your will.
Never let my cup rest after just having its fill.
I give myself unreservedly
For, I know I never deserved thee.
Yet, You reached for a seed of life buried,
That You might grow and entwine it to You faithfully.
This tower of strength was made strong by my weakness.
For, it is there, yielded, that You are perfected.

Shortly after I turned 30, on the first of October, 2012, the Lord began speaking with me concerning my season at my current place of employment. He said it had come to an end. When I asked Him about direction as to where I should go, He began to talk with me, night after night, about beginning a business for myself. He spoke to me in a way I could not even try to tune out.

He was so clear, so loud, that I finally said, "I hear you, Lord, and I won't deny Your voice. I will name this business after You so I will always remember it is You who worked this out in me."

The song about the Lord being our high tower of refuge continuously played in my spirit, over and over again. It was the sound of my spirit singing to the Lord; and, all I could do is take the leap of faith and trust Christ. This poem came during that point.

***Ecclesiastes 3:15** That which is now already has been, and that which is to be already has been: and God seeks that which has already passed by.*

The Keeper Of The Marrow
(November 2, 2012)

You are the keeper of the marrow.
The prudent grace on the dawn of the lion.
You are the scarlet letters of love
Embroidered within the fragments of a once wounded soul.
You are a fragrance,
A delight for the earth to dwell in.
You are the safety
Of a hundred thousand wings
Over the little lamb.
You are the thunder
Cracking plates of temporal drifts.
You are radiance dawning
From within darkened rifts.
I see the twinkling of a flower
When moisture sparks the hues.
The delight of a morning's rose
Caressed in perfume from the dew.
You are the vine and trellis — both You are.
A foundation to cling to,
An ascend towards something new.
You are my story.
For, from before time,
You, too, were already mine.

This poem really came from time communing in the presence of Christ. I was pondering on a message my Pastor had shared about all the names of God; and, that we can draw on each one of those names in every encounter and circumstance in life. I realized how much I desired to know intimately His names and learn more of who He is to me and in me.

An Awakening Mother's Prayer
(*November 30, 2012*)

Humbled do I come to You, Oh Sovereign One.
For, I am broken and as tender as the dawn.
Wishful thinking cannot carry me,
Only the comfort of Your fleece.
Vanguards echo remorse softly.
Shattered pieces of comfort elude me.
For, in old, they were vain and in pretend.
This heart, Oh Lord, do mend.
Drive the prisms of smoke from me.
Give me the courage and strength
To be the mother these boys need me to be.
Mend, too, the fragments of my soul,
So, that in turn, my sons, too, shall be whole.
Remove the cartooned imaginations from their world around.
That Your truth may pierce through the disillusioned ground.
The call within them is crying out,
"Be our stream, Lord, here in this drought."

When my youngest son went into the hospital, this poem came as a prayer. I realized more and more that the healing of our children must begin with us. As I spoke with my Father's Spirit, I began to understand layers of wasted energy that should have been invested in my children.

Ecclesiastes 2:11 Then I looked on all that my hands had done and the labor I had spent in doing it, and behold, all was vanity and a striving after the wind and a feeding on it, and there was no profit under the sun. I then realized that Vanity is only a perception.

It is our understanding of who we are. Vanity tries to peel back the layer of a wound and disguise itself as ointment to a sore. Really, all it is doing within us is creating another barrier to the real you.

50

Pearl Of Price
(December 10, 2012)

Here I am as dust placed back upon the ground.
All words You gave me feed I now on those profound.
I ponder on Your ancient mysteries,
And in this present desire, I Your Spirit to please.
I choose You above the silver
And wretched gems that make flesh quiver.
I choose You to be my beloved,
Unchanging and relationally interrupted.
I choose You, Oh Pearl of Price.

I finally understood what my Pastor meant by 'we sell all and forsake all, when we find that pearl of great price.' Christ is truly my Pearl of Great Price.

Unto You, My Love
(December 16, 2012)

I shall write unto You, my Love,
My affection, Oh apple of my eye, and desire of my being.
Ask of me what You will and
Allow me to offer my sacrifice unto You.
I shall be who You've created me to be.
I shall speak as an oracle of Your Spirit,
I shall love as You commanded me to.
I shall allow You to blossom within me.
I shall not walk by fear, or by sight,
But, by Your Spirit for it works deep within me.

An Ode To The Soul From The Spirit
(December 20, 2012)

Oh, breath of existence where did you waste away?
Oh, fragrance of incense to where doth your love play?
You frolic in the hills of desire, in vividly colored dreams,
And, as loose woman's hire, trade your life for just the means.
You caress the fields of plenty, never tasting the all in all.
You forsook gold for a penny,
For, it was deception who first made the call.
Oh, army of awry lovers,
Selling birthrights for moments of bliss.
Our nakedness now uncovers
The betrayal of each choice's kiss.

So, here we weep in judgment,
Our coin purse thrown aside.
Eternal vapors now pungent,
As our inner conscious now tries to hide.
Yet, we must face our self,
The cheap whore we hid away.
For, victory sits upon a shelf,
While we weigh the cost of what we must pay.

Arise and shine, oh church!
Called long from before time.
In midnight hours of loneliness,
The void within does seek and search.
Satisfaction is not a jewel befitting a royal priest.
For, it is a cry of the duel of soul and flesh, it is a yeast.
We must allow the turning of sediments that come to a boil.
Refinement is a fire that cleans us lest we spoil.

"If we are not about our Father's business, then, we are wasting the breath of our existence."
— *Pastor Linda Darnell*

Over the past several years, I was literally cut away from a former life, associations of past acquaintances, politically correct friendships, and, even former mentors of one sort or another.

It was prophesied to me that I would be led by green pastures, though, I had yet to learn what that really meant. Now, Christ, the very indwelling of the presence of God, has become those pastures to me. Through the shifting and breaking away I have undergone over the past few years, the Lord began to speak this to my spirit:

Either we cut the umbilical cords of former thoughts and dreams or we shall be diseased by the unclean food we are still eating (food meaning our thoughts). Be cautious and aware by whose table you sit – what you allow your ears to hear and what words forsake the covenant of Christ within you by allowing your mind to wander towards it unaware. For, you shall come into agreement with that strife and division. Watchmen, stand guard. Guard that precious pearl of Christ within you at all cost. We are in the day of our security blankets being torn off and our inner lewdness exposed. Our inward nakedness is truly a place of humility. It is also the place where our weaknesses are exposed, that Christ may take over that yielded layer and truly begin to heal us, restore us, and deliver us for good. Line upon line, precept upon precept.

Isaiah 28:9-11 *Whom shall he teach knowledge? and whom shall he make to understand doctrine? them that are weaned from the milk, and drawn from the breasts. For precept must be upon precept, precept upon precept; line upon line, line upon line; here a little, and there a little: For with stammering lips and another tongue will he speak to this people.*

Made in the USA
Charleston, SC
26 March 2013